Pundemonium
Vol. 3

James E. Larson

Lefse Press—Agoura Hills, Ca
ISBN: 979-8-9874392-4-1
eBook ISBN: 979-8-9874392-5-8
Title: *Pundemonium Vol. 3*
Author: James E. Larson
Digital distribution | 2023
Paperback | 2023

Dedication

The author dedicates this book to his loving family, wife Cindy, daughter Erica, and son Greg. They have had to listen to the author over the years trying out the various puns on them. They deserve recognition for enduring that pun-ishment.

Chapter One

A woman discovered seeds in her orange drink she got from a can that was from an orange drink factory. She didn't like that and sued the factory. In court, a lawyer for the factory started yelling at her on the stand and the judge did not like that. Therefore, in the end, because of the seeds in the drink, the judge also issued a restraining order to the owner of the factory.

In a trial, the case was about a writer who was hired without a contract to write a musical poem for a singer. The poem was written and delivered but the singer did not pay for it. The jury found the money for the poem was ode to the writer.

In France, a carpenter built a staircase for a client. The staircase had a missing step and the client fell down because of it and broke his leg. In America, that case would result in a major lawsuit. In France, that incident of a missing step was just a faux pas.

A cowboy was always bragging about the metal object attached to the heel of his cowboy boots. He said they were solid gold. A claim that everyone around him thought was spurious.

John and Kate were dating, however, they came to a fork in the road and decided to split up. Kate was having a hard time saying goodbye, so John thought it was time to step in and say bifurcate.

In the Himalayas, in Asia, I heard the Abominable Snowman and Sasquatch agreed to be in a race to see who was the fastest. The Abominable Snowman had a sore ankle and Yeti still won.

An arrogant electrician who was less than 5' tall, thought he knew everything about the flow of electricity. However, when he was rushing to fix a problem, the flow of electricity went in the opposite way it was supposed to go. It seems he was always coming up with a short delay.

Chapter Two

A used car salesman wanted to make a career change so he went to work for a carpenter that constructs stairs in new homes. The former salesman thought this change in careers was a step in the right direction.

When an immigrant farmer was looking for land to settle, he chose the small wooded valleys rather than the large open flat areas of land. He thought there was more game and water in the small wooded valleys. He always liked to say, "Far more in the Dell!"

The leading male actor in the movie "Breakfast at Tiffany's" always had as his motto, "Be Preppard."

There was a rumor around years ago that after the success of the television show "Gidget," about a diminutive beach girl, the producers wanted a spin off show about her sister. Her sister was described as restless, nervous and uneasy. They were going to call the television show "Fidget."

In Europe, somebody ranked the top ten nudist camps according to their popularity, one to ten, one being best. Alas number ten was ranked at the bottom of the bare all.

In Arizona, a home owner was complaining about the smell coming from his roof. An exterminator was called and he found some animal droppings on the roof. The exterminator was quoted telling the client, it's just like the old movie says, it was "Scat on a Hot Tin Roof."

A veterinarian who was dealing with a small sick song bird. He gave the bird a pill that was kind of acidic. He noted in his ledger that it was a bitter pill to swallow.

A person thought he was going to be cast in a movie that was going to be directed by his hairdresser. While he was in the makeup chair for the movie, he found out he only would have one line. Also, he did not like that the hairdresser was combing his hair and the hair barely had a crease down the middle of his hair. He walked away from the movie because the hair dresser would not give him a bigger part.

Chapter Three

In London, a gardener named Frank, got into a noisy argument with a fellow gardener while working in the community garden. Frank found out he could not get rid of weeds and argue at the same time. You see, it was too much of a tough row to hoe.

A cookie dough addict admitted that he kneads the dough every day.

An arrogant old carpenter, who makes wood supports for rafter joists, just makes his supports and struts around all day.

An old politician, who owned a very young female horse, realized his young horse was very wild and would break all kinds of things. He thought he should sell it. He was just another politician who wanted to get rid of a filly buster.

A tire company executive was transferred to London and when he landed, he was told the company already had a place ready for him to live. He was in the country only a few minutes and driving to the place when he discovered he already had a flat.

Speaking of gimmicks, an up and coming mischievous hip-hop singer would come on stage with a vest covered in fresh young onions. He wanted to be known as the original "Rapscallion."

A local Rabbi, who was a baseball fan, was thinking of ways to do good deeds for the community. He came up with the idea of giving to the local little league baseball players who are catchers free catcher's gloves. He thought that would be a good 'mittsva.'

A new worker in a mannequin factory was making just the lower limbs for the day and he was putting them all in an overcrowded container. His boss saw this and told him, "Don't put all your legs in one basket!"

In a contest between a football quarterback and a soccer player as to who could make a ball go the farthest, the soccer player won hands down.

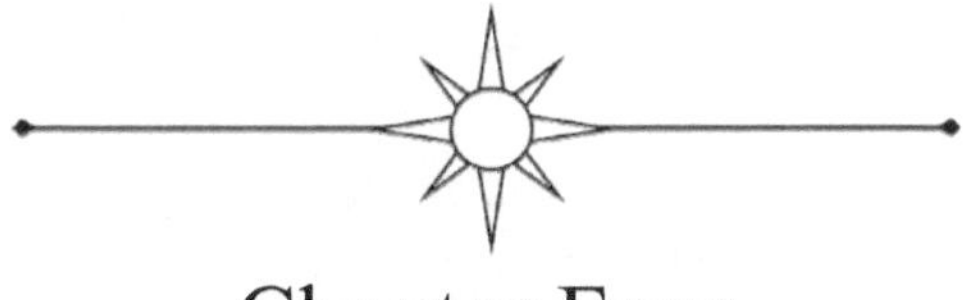

Chapter Four

Two world travelers, who always paid for their own meals, were thinking about becoming citizens of Holland. They went out to a restaurant in the City of Rotterdam. During the dinner they decided they did not want to be citizens of the county because they hated the food they were served. They suddenly got in an argument and wanted the other person to pay for their meal. So by the time it came to pay, neither one wanted to go Dutch!

An angry politician in South America, who was a big dog lover, was getting ready to start a revolution to over throw the government in his country. He was going to train dogs to storm the capital, but in the end he could only find three dogs. Most people thought that concerning the revolution, he really screwed the putsch!

In a small Oregon town there is a very small university that only teach two courses. One course is about the different kind of containers that hold different kinds of liquids and the other course is all about social etiquette. The university is proudly known by the locals as Tank U!

In Havana, I heard a person was hit by a very large five pound cigar that had been filled with marijuana. The hospital listed his injury was caused by blunt trauma.

A big fireworks show was reviewed by a critic for a local newspaper. The critic did not like the show and wrote a bad review. The fireworks were mentioned in the bad review as just a flash in the pan.

A practicing dentist always wanted to open a motorcycle shop that also leases helicopters. It seems he just cannot get enough of working with choppers.

A farmer in California growing just parsley, was very strict with the number of plants to be picked by a worker each day. The farmer said that if the workers don't pick their quota of parsley, he would garnish their wages.

An old NBA basketball star was remembering all the times he spent dunking the ball around the basketball hoop. He was riminiscing about the good old days.

Chapter Five

I heard some Catholic parishioners were being denied the right to sit in their pews during the period leading up to Easter because they were found to be sleeping during the church services. So because of that infraction, somnolent.

Old time movie film editors used to do everything in reel time.

The owner of a factory that makes the wooden objects you knock down when you are bowling, also makes the sharp pointed items you use to sew clothes. The owner happens to be the nervous type because he is always on pins and needles.

They tell me that removing the very large, dirty, smelly underground containers that are used for gas storage under old gas stations is a tankless job.

I heard the Navy was designing new barracks for the new female recruits. The finished design had a bathroom directly over the lower floor room which is going to be used as a place where the recruits could store their fancy civilian footwear. You could say the Navy went 'Head over Heels' on this design.

At a small circus in the South, an animal trainer has an act with ducks that do all kinds of tricks and are then rewarded with slices of Velveeta. The local paper named the act "Cheese and Quackers."

In South Dakota, a farmer, who leases land from his landlord, was told by the landlord he was required to grow only hemp. The farmer signed the lease but about the requirement, he said he felt he was sort of roped into it.

The dictator of North Korea, it is said, always tries to stay Un top of everything in his country.

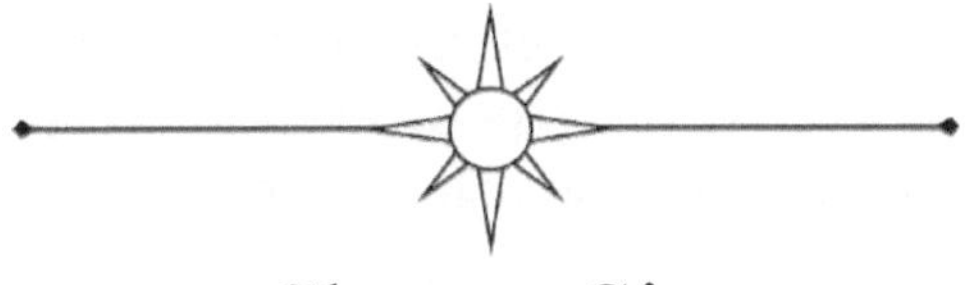

Chapter Six

The owner of a paper manufacturing company noticed that one of his employees was sending out packets of paper that had less sheets than the industry standard. The owner reamed out the employee for that.

At a retirement dinner for one of his workers, a leather shop owner gave a speech about the employee. The owner also explained that it was a custom at this shop that retiring workers, in a symbolic gesture, would give back to the boss one of his tools he used all those years. The owner went on to say, "He was the best worker and he gave me his awl."

For a trade show, an auto muffler company built a huge scale model of a muffler you could walk through. The worker who made it stayed up all night before the show to finish it. When he walked through it from beginning to the end of the model, he said he felt exhausted.

A soup company that was concerned about employee theft recently instituted some new rules when employees leave the room where the soup is made. When they leave that room, they are all required to take what the employees call a brothalyzer test.

A highly sought after doctor in Beverly Hills only operates on celebrities that need treatment on their major leg joint located between their upper and lower legs. He is usually discreet about who he operates on but once in a while he will tell some reporter on a kneed to know basis.

I remember taking a tour in an old museum in London, where there were weapons from a long time ago before there were explosives. One weapon looked much like a teeter totter with a spear that launches on one end and on the other end is a place where a person would jump from a height then sit down forcefully with their arse sticking out to launch the spear. I think the guide said that could be the reason that from then on a collection of weapons is called an arsenal.

The owner of a factory that makes the thick covering that are put over sheets on beds was talking to the press. He said he considered his coverings the best. Of course, he was making a blanket statement.

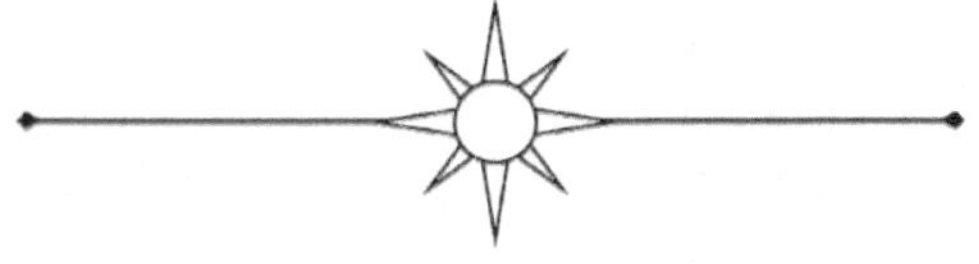

Chapter Seven

You know, it makes sense that people who get their electric cars charged up would have to pay for that service with something called currency.

A farmer in the South taught a cow to sort of sing songs. The cow's favorite songs are a version of Glenn Miller's song "In the Moooooed" and a version of David Bowie's song "Udder Pressure."

They are drawing up plans for a new factory in Ohio that will make home appliances that you use to press your clothes. They are now ironing out the details.

An old gorilla, who knew a lot of tricks, was retiring from a small circus in the South. So the trainer put a young gorilla in the old gorilla's cage. He thought the young gorilla could watch the old gorilla do his tricks and the young gorilla would get excited and just ape him.

Did you know that the lawyer that checks all the copyright issues for all of Ian Flemming's movies about his super spy has to be licensed and insured? Of course, he was also Bonded.

In Texas, a bored and broke man decided on a whim he would start a dating service for chickens. He said he was just trying to make hens meet.

A writing pen manufacturing company was having a contest where the company asked their employees to come up with an exciting name for their new pen. When they submitted their names on a piece of paper, the company said the second to the last entry name was chosen and it was "Penultimate!"

There is a rumor going around that someone in the band Aerosmith is going to write a Chinese cookbook called, "Wok This Way."

Chapter Eight

When a lawn gets a coat of moisture in the morning, and then another one later, is that an example of dewplication?

A tent salesman was looking at a map of house addresses and wondering how many households would buy a tent. He really wanted to canvas the neighborhood.

A rabbit farmer in Ohio that was having big problems selling his farm, chose to dwell on the small problem of him trying to keep some rabbit couples apart during mating season. Do you think all the farmer was doing was splitting hares?

A pastor in a small town in Kentucky had a one dollar per occasion swear jar for his flock. The money in the jar was stuck at 143 dollars. Suddenly, a congregant came in the church, told the pastor what he had said, and then put a dollar in the jar. The pastor said, "Well, he just laid a gross number on me!"

In Italy, I heard about an artist who made a sculpture of just the head and shoulders of a famous person but the finished sculpture was not very good. The whole thing was a total bust.

A farmer in Iowa had such a high yield of corn that he had just harvested. He sold some of it to a new factory that was experimenting with grinding up the corn and adding it to other materials to produce the items on a car that protect it on the front and the rear. When the farmer was asked about selling his extra corn to that factory, he said, "What else would you do with a bumper crop?"

Science is still trying to figure this one out...if the sound of a horn on a train changes from high frequency to low frequency when the train passes a stationary bystander and the same thing happens five minutes later...are those two sounds considered to be an example of a dopplerganger?

A perfume company has come out with a new perfume for men who are overly obsessive with their clothes and appearance. The perfume is called Fopbrege.

Chapter Nine

The keynote speaker at a convention in Norway that was extolling the advantages of whale meat, keep blubbering on.

In Poland, at a window manufacturing company, a quality control inspector on the assembly line had to run his hand over every piece of glass to see if the glass was entirely smooth. The inspector complained that the assembly line was moving too fast giving him a headache and he asked for help. A friendly co-worker nearby came over and offered to help. The co-worker said, "I can feel your pane..."

In Louisiana, a woman named Annette had a fishing show on the local TV. It was called, "Casting with Annette!"

In a small town in Utah, there is a woman that has an office where she does spinal manipulations on her patients backs and as a wonderful singer, she also trains singers to sing in their church's groups. She calls herself a "Choirpractor."

A psychologist had a new patient that thought he was a skunk. She did not want to aggravate the new patient or otherwise he might raise a big stink.

A fruit salesman, who was also a juggler, would always do his act with aplomb.

Certain old German cars who are retired, often end up in the Old Volks Home.

A high school band conductor had one disruptive clarinet player that always seemed to have problems putting her clarinet together. One day the conductor had enough and started to reed her the riot act.

To this day, the Patriot who in 1776, rode through the streets of Boston to warn the British were coming, will always be Revered.

Chapter Ten

A young apprentice on a wooden ship long ago, was told to work on the hull of the ship. He looked around and pointed to the piece of wood at the rear of the ship that steers the ship. He blurted out, "I would rudder work on that!"

Little known fact, there is a sort of secret dental school where they graduate the finest dentists in the USA. The school is known as "TOP GUM."

Did you know there is a long list of people who want to learn how to drive "Oscar Mayer's Wienermobile?" The people in charge have to find those who can cut the mustard.

A big game hunter in India was hired by a TV station to capture a tiger that had escaped from a local zoo. The tiger was last seen in a neighborhood that had many vegetable gardens. The hunter captured the tiger in one of those gardens and the TV station got it on film. The TV station interviewed the hunter and he said, "I caught a tiger by the kale, it's plain to see!"

In a village in Germany, a woman named Mercedes had a bad back problem from working for a car company she wanted to keep secret. She went to a chiropractor who helped her a lot. The chiropractor was so happy about that that she told the whole village about the healing and also where she worked. Now, the whole village knows Mercedes bends.

A tourist went to a strange eating place off the beaten path. He ate some deep fried fritters and went back to the ship. He got real sick. A passerby asked him what did he eat and how does he feel? The tourist said in answer to both questions, "I falafel!"

I heard some mathematician trained his parrot to say "2 + 2 = 4" over and over again. Now there is an example of adnauseam!

The son of a pastor just knew that he too would become a pastor as the son finished his studies. The son was preordained.

Chapter Eleven

A person who can recite all the different land shapes and forms on the earth surface might be considered a knoll-it-all.

Early explorers discovered the large vast Russian grasslands in lower Russia steppe by steppe.

Judges of the West Virginia Tobacco Spitting Contest, at the local county fair, were going to rate the contestants from one to ten. A judge, and former contestant, was asked about the amounts of tobacco the contestants had to spit out and he said, "That's the normal amount around here...it's what I would expectorate."

An artist called Tom in Atlanta, was just fixated on the shape of the number four. So he made a twenty foot high number four and installed it in his rear yard. The shade from the sculpture caused the neighbors vegetable garden to fail and so the neighbor sued Tom. The judge said it was an easy case of where the sculpture four shadowed the demise of the garden.

They say drilling for oil is a boring job.

I heard the world's tallest man years ago ended up with size 22 shoes. Everybody thought that was some feat.

They were tearing down the old church and auctioning off different parts of the building. One bidder had his eye on the church bell, but he thought it might cost to much. The auctioneer said he would try to help him out. The auctioneer said, "If you buy the steeple, you will get the belfry."

Strangely enough, there is a farmer in Iowa who has a cow that has acquired a taste for coffee. He gives her coffee only after she gives birth. The farmer's veterinarian insists that it be decalfeinated.

Chapter Twelve

A synagogue was having a masquerade party. A person was trying to find another person who could fit in the front of the horse costume to complete the costume. The person he chose was the one person who blows the Shofar because he already knew how to Cantor.

A Rabbi was asked about how the blowing of the ram's horn was going during the services. He said, "Shofar, so good!"

The joke goes Dracula was at the counter of a blood bank at the local hospital. He asked the staff how much blood is stored in the vault. Dracula then winked at the staff and said, "I'm asking for a fiend."

Is it any wonder that the study of large, wet, slimy fish is called Ichthyology?

Thinking about writing a new kind of lengthy book is a novel idea.

A German farmer bragged that his potatoes were the best in Europe. He put a label on his bags of potatoes that said, "Tuber Alles!"

A long time ago in a Bavarian village, there was a young bawdy woman whose face was shaped like a crescent moon and she also sold hand tools on the side. Everybody called her a "Crescent Wench."

I once heard there was an ancient civilization that worshiped pottery and thought the people who made them were Gods. There was a law that if a pot cracked and fell to the floor in pieces, before they could repair the pottery, the Gods would have to notify the next of kiln.

If you think denial is a river in Egypt, then what the fish in that river would nibble on could be up for debate.

Young pioneers on the Oregon Trail could not wait until their parents changed to a gentler soap for their baths and that's no lye.

Chapter Thirteen

A flea circus was scheduled to appear at a famous venue, but at the last moment, it was scratched from the program.

In Australia, there is a park where you can ride on a large, flightless bird. It is called an Emusment Park.

A duck farmer was trying to buy some land from another duck farmer. The buyer was offering the seller a down payment. The seller said, "No thanks, I would rather have cash!"

A long time stamp collector was bidding against another stamp collector for a very rare stamp. The long time stamp collector lost the bid and he said, "I know what it is like to be licked!"

A not so bright young mechanic was on his first day on the job at an auto repair shop fixing tires and things that stop the car. The boss walked by and told the mechanic to take a break. The boss spent the rest of the day trying to find the missing brake.

A community garden club in England was having a carnival type fundraiser. One game was throwing a certain herb, that was made into a ball, through a hole in the wall to win. A participant enjoyed this game and was at this game a long time. He suddenly realized that and said out loud, "Thyme flies when you are having fun!"

A fire eater at a carnival decided to show everyone his act. He would mix his mucus with a sip of gasoline and spit it out and then light it on fire. The local newspaper described his act as "Phlegmboyant!"

The Javelin Catching competition never really caught on at the Olympics. The Olympics Committee made a point of that.

A graduate of the large Catholic University near South Bend, Indiana had just become president of a large company he was hired for at the mail room level years ago. When asked if he ever imagined that he would be president when he started years ago, he said, "I had a hunch back at Notre Dame."

Chapter Fourteen

A man was arrested in Los Angeles the other day. He was hiding his brother, who was wanted by the police, in his rear yard in a garden structure surrounded by trees and shrubs. They arrested him for arbouring a fugitive.

The employees at a rug company were planning to go on strike. They were not sure when, but it was looming right in front of them.

A goofy and foolish clown in a circus publicly stated he thought he was the best clown in the circus. All the other clowns just thought he was supercilious.

There was a family in Europe who liked to play lawn games. Unfortunately, they lived in a treeless desert without any wood to make things to play with. So they substituted any wood required ball item with balls of yarn. The game was to knock balls of yard through small wire hoops. The family called their own little game "Crochet."

Neighbor Tom was so mad at his neighbor for his trees dropping all their leaves on Tom's property. Tom was going to cuss him out verbally, but decided the better thing to do was write him an angry letter. Tom was still so upset so the letter had to be all cursive.

An old English scholar asked his butler to bring him a cup of tea and a copy of the Canterbury Tales book. The scholar said he likes to set by the fireplace with his cup and Chaucer by his side.

A group of rookie hockey players were on the rink playing in a minor league game. Someone in the stands threw a perfectly round cake on the rink. One player hit it between his legs from one end of the rink to the other without anyone touching it. A referee saw that trick shot and said that shot was "Icing on the cake!"

In the old days, a street car company thought it was a good public relations move to hire a young woman to sit on a street car and to only collect fares. It really was just a token job.

Chapter Fifteen

Not many know this, but I heard sharks are often time friendly with other sharks. They like to chum around with other sharks behind an ocean going fishing boat.

It is only fitting that Arnold Ziffel, the pig, who was featured on the TV show "Green Acres," wanted to be the center of attention when he was highlighted on the show. He just naturally wanted to hog the spotlight!

The producer of a local TV baseball show stated he did not want any moving texts at the bottom of the TV screen while a sportscaster was on the TV. He explained that he agreed with the Tom Hanks character in the movie 'A League of Their Own' when he said, "There's no chyron in baseball!"

I heard there is a company in the capital city of the Philippines that will only accept mail if it is in a manila envelope.

When a contractor received a change order from the architect concerning a certain front part of a church he was remodeling, he knew he was going to alter the look of it.

Little Bobby's retention of history information in his elementary school class was pretty poor. His history lessons would go in one era and out the other.

An old worker at a carpet factory who was in charge of aligning the rug fibers in a certain way, got very tired so he left work and took his work home. It was good he had a benevolent employer that let him go home and take his nap.

I heard the McDonald's Hamburglar was interrogated because of his behavior towards Ronald McDonald. The Hamburglar was grilled over that relationship.

Did you know that a famous astrological newspaper was the first newspaper to have a comets section?

Chapter Sixteen

There was a robbery at a dress factory. The police thought it was an inside job. The suspect had only been working on the factory floor less than a day and had only added vertical creases to only four skirts. The police questioned him on the factory floor and asked him if he would like to make a statement. He said no, turned to the skirt in front of him and pleated the fifth.

A person was trying to decide if he wanted to buy into a pancake franchise or a breakfast house franchise. He thought he had picked the pancake franchise, but then he second thoughts and he started to waffle.

A farmer in Florida hired an unknown company to drain a swamp on his land. That company really did not know what it was doing and right away it got bogged down.

A seamstress at a shirt factory was in charge of designing the bit of fabric that is located at the end of a shirt sleeve and that covers your wrist. She was so good at it that she ended up living off the cuff.

A dairy farmer in Wisconsin was advertising the sale of one of his cows. He said it was one of his best cows with high production numbers. A potential buyer did some investigating and found out the seller was exaggerating the numbers. As for the potential deal, the seller with the cow was milking it.

Is someone who loves a certain kind of pickle without knowing the history and background of that particular pickle a dill-ettante?

A man went into a store to buy an electric razor but when he got there, he thought the prices were kind of high. So the man told the owner and the owner said, "I happen to be in a good mood, how about I shave a little off the price?"

A leather store in New York was advertising a small traveling bag that had an electronic device on it that you could communicate with it to help you find it if you lost it. Also, the store went on to say, if the bag is stolen, be sure to call the valise.

Chapter Seventeen

The old chef was telling the young chef about his life and how he had spent some time in jail years ago. As the young chef was cooking and adding little round green seasonings from a plant in the Mediterranean area, the old chef kept talking about the capers he had in his life.

An old boxer, with his time piece in his hand, walked into a watch repair store and said to the very small young clerk, "I want you to clean my clock!"

The clerk stammered and said, "Sir, I don't think I am in your weight class!"

In the continuing adoration of all things bacon, the owner of a small vineyard in California adds a few drops of bacon juice to their wine bottles. The owner calls his new concoction 'Swine' and he thinks you will never get boared by the taste.

There is a factory that makes small ornamental mats made of lace or paper with a lace pattern that can be placed on a plate. The employees have to listen over the intercom once a day to messages from the company president who praises the item the factory is producing. These are their doily affirmations.

A group of beer company workers had worked all morning drawing up plans to add a large new building next to their existing building. Now they said they needed a break. They knew what kind beer they liked and that they also had to keep working because of a deadline. So to meet both of their requirements, they spent the rest of the day at the draft table.

A couple of old buddies went into a shoe store to buy some shoes. This particular shoe store liked to ask customers about their life styles and then suggest what kind of shoe would fit their life style. One of the buddies said they just like to sit on the sofa all day and watch TV. "Ah," said the shoe clerk, "a pair of loafers!"

At Christmas time, a farmer in Iowa has a display down by the road at the end of his driveway. His display is a Christmas tree with ears of corn hanging all over it. He sells his ears of corn to naive city dwellers as Christmas "cornaments."

After just two days, a young worker at a leather tannery shop could not handle the smells and so he was going to quit. He tried to keep it a secret but with his constant complaining, he just gave up trying to hide it.

About the Author

The author, James E. Larson, has always enjoyed a good pun. Just recently, he decided to create new ones for a book. He says like anything else, some puns come easy while other need some rewrites before they are finished. A good pun needs a good back story that sets up the 'Pun-ch Line.' That is the fun part of creating puns.